D1617359

Zone Journals

ZONE
JOURNALS

CHARLES
WRIGHT

Farrar / Straus / Giroux

New York

Library of Congress Cataloging-in-Publication Data
Wright, Charles.
Zone journals.
"The first five poems appeared in . . . limited
edition volume entitled 5 journals"—
I. Wright, Charles. 5 journals.
II. Title.
PS3573.R52Z59   1988   811'.54   07-21207

Acknowledgments are made to Field, The Paris Review,
The Yale Review, Open Places, The Gettysburg Review,
and A Celebration for Stanley Kunitz, where some of these
poems originally appeared. "Yard Journal" and sections
of "A Journal of the Year of the Ox" originally appeared
in The New Yorker; other sections of "A Journal of the
Year of the Ox" were first published in Ploughshares. The
first five poems appeared in a fine press, limited edition
volume entitled 5 Journals, printed and published by
Red Ozier Press, New York City, 1986.

For Glenn Gould and Merle Travis

Contents

𝕣𝕖

𝕣𝕖

𝕣𝕖

𝕣𝕖

Yard Journal

—Mist in the trees, and soiled water and grass cuttings splotch
The driveway,
afternoon starting to bulk up in the west
A couple of hours down the road:
Strange how the light hubs out and wheels
concentrically back and forth
After a rain, as though the seen world
Quavered inside a water bead
swung from a grass blade:
The past is never the past:
it lies like a long tongue
We walk down into the moist mouth of the future, where new
    teeth
Nod like new stars around us,
And winds that itch us, and plague our ears,
sound curiously like the old songs.

—Deep dusk and lightning bugs
alphabetize on the east wall,
The carapace of the sky blue-ribbed and buzzing
Somehow outside it all,
Trees dissolving against the night's job,
houses melting in air:
Somewhere out there an image is biding its time,
Burning like Abraham in the cold, swept
expanses of heaven,

Waiting to take me in and complete my equation:
What matters is abstract, and is what love is,
Candescent inside the memory,
                              continuous
And unexpungable, as love is . . .

   Bluo jay'o bound liko a kangaroo'o in tho lawn'o high graoo,
Then up in a brushstroke
                        and over the hedge in one arc.
Light on lights downn the aealia plants,
Yesterday's cloud banks entrescoed still
                                   just under the sky's cornice,
Cardinal quick transfusion into the green arm of the afternoon.
Wax-like flowers of sunlight drift
                           through the dwarf orchard and float
Under the pygmied peaches and pears
All over America,
                 and here, too, the blossoms
Continuing down from nowhere, out of the blue.
The mockingbird's shadow is burned in the red clay below him.

—Exclusion's the secret: what's missing is what appears
Most visible to the eye:
                        the more luminous anything is,
The more it subtracts what's around it,
Peeling away the burned skin of the world
                                   making the unseen seen:
Body by new body they all rise into the light
Tactile and still damp,
That rhododendron and dogwood tree, that spruce,
An architecture of absence,
                           a landscape whose words

4

Are imprints, dissolving images after the eyelids close:
I take them away to keep them there—
                    that hedgehorn, for instance, that stalk . . .

—A bumblebee the size of my thumb
                              rises like Geryon
From the hard Dantescan gloom
Under my window sash to lip the rain gutter's tin *bolgia*,
Then backs out like a hummingbird
                              spiraling languidly out of sight,
Shoulders I've wanted to sit on, a ride I've wanted to take,
Deposited into the underlight
                              of cities thronged in the grass,
Fitful illuminations, iron-colored plain that lies
Littered with music and low fires,
                              stone edge of the pit
At the end of every road,
First faces starting to swim up:
                              Bico, my man, are you here?

A Journal of English Days

                                        (September)
—Kensington Church Walk, St. Mary Abbots
Gray stone and dun through the mustard edges of chestnut leaves.
Inside, a funeral's going on and I back off
To sit on a wooden bench
Against a brick wall
                    in the slick, unseasonable sunshine,
Trying to piece together
The way it must have been for someone in 1908
Fresh up from Italy,
A couple of books of his own poems in one hand
                                        and a dead galaxy
Set to go off in crystal inside his head.
Over the stained-glass windows in front of me,
In Kensington black and white,
                    Ancient Lights
Is nailed to the churchside stone,
The children trailing out of the false penumbra
                                into the sun-screed in Indian file
Then in again, shrilling, in cadence, their little song.

—I'm back for a second look,
                    but someone is meditating on last week's bench
In a full lotus. Now he touches his nose
With his right forefinger, and now
With his left.
                    His black shoes puddle beneath him

6

Like backs of mirrors he'll walk on tenderly
Over the flat-laid churchyard gravestones when he leaves.
But now he's back in position,
                    hands cupped
In his lap, thumb end touching thumb end, his eyes closed—

One of those weightless, effortless late September days
As sycamore leaves
                    tuck down the unresisting air
Onto the fire-knots of late roses
Still pumping their petals of flame
                    up from the English loam,
And I suddenly recognize
The difference between the spirit and flesh
                    is finite, and slowly transgressable . . .

                                        (October)

—October everywhere out of the sunlight
Onto the China jade of the blowing fields
Of Kensington Gardens—
                    or else come down like wet lint
Over the Avon, soaking the glass.
It swivels my eyes that work me for grief and affliction
And pink my spirit, it guides my hand.

Fulke Greville lies in his stone boat in the church of St. Mary
In Warwickshire, not rippling the cold
Which clings like water drops to what was his face
On the other side of the light.

His kinsmen, Lords of the Bear and the Ragged Staff,
                                        lie scattered around him,

Hermetically sealed in stone,
Who was friend to Elizabeth R and Sir Philip Sidney, ghost
In his own room now,
                    all passions heeled.

This afternoon I came up
Out of his Warwick dungeon

                         into the slow swish of the English rain,
Its bead curtain and lengths of chain
Strangely consoling after the iron artifacts
Hanging below like rib cages
                         and lungs in the torturous gloom.

The castle seemed to encircle me with its stone wings
And all of it lift
                    slightly at once, then settle back
As though the wind had died
That blows continuously under our feet
Holding up everything, then started again,
                         and what had sunk was risen,
I don't know, at least to where it began . . .

—October's a kind time,
The rain lying like loose bandages over the ground,
The white bounty of mushrooms thrusting their flesh up,
The comforting slide of darkness
                         edging like deep water
Back through the afternoon.
The sycamore trees in Lennox Gardens crisp and spray
In the wind, our discontent,
                    like Orpheus, singing elsewhere,
Charon, in slow motion, poling his empty boat

Cross-current, over the dark water
Into the different music of London traffic,
                              the coin still clenched in his teeth
The other side of the Thames . . .

Back in the Gardens, it's tag end of a skitterish day,
October 17, Sir Philip dead
397 years today,
I watch the stiff papers scudding across the lawn,
Leaves heaped to vindicate speedily
The offices of the end,
                    dogs nosing the moist-eared edges of things,
Noticing gradually
A larger darkness inching up through the dark
Like grass, that means to cover us all.
Across the way, the yellow moths of the window lights
Break from their blue cocoons.

—The trees stay green longer here, lacking
The clubbing frost that stuns them to glory.
                              Their leaves lie in limes and tans
Flocking the grass, vaguely pre-Cubist to me,
And blurred, without my glasses, arranged
In an almost-pattern of colors across the yard,
The same colors Cézanne once used in the same way
So often down in Provence.
                    He died there today
Seventy-seven years ago, October 22, the fields and houses and trees
Still these colors and pure arrangements
Oozing out of the earth, dropping out of the sky
                              in memory of him each year
Everywhere, north and south . . .

9

He never painted the moon.
Never romantic enough,
                         he saw what he saw in a white light.
Still, I remember it there, hanging like a doubloon
Over Puyricard, outside Aix, some fifteen years ago,
Godfrey and I in our yellow suits
                         vampling the landscape
Along the canal, first in its half, then two weeks later ito full droon.
It's here now, powdering through the trees
                         in cuay go by, und drinkin ning in the sloat
The blue light from a TV swarms at the windowpanes
In one of the Dutch Georgians across the way.
He made us see differently, where the hooks fit, and the eyes go . . .
Nothing is ever finished.

—Up from the basement flat at 43A,
                         up past the Greek college,
Across Walton to Ovington Gardens
Then over to Brompton Road
And across,
            left to the Oratory and right
Up under the chestnut trees to Ennismore Mews,
Up past the gardens and Prince's Gate
Across the main road and Rotten Row,
                         bicycle track
And long grass down to the Serpentine,
Ducks on the water, geese on the water, the paired swans
Imperious and the gulls
                         neat on the slick edges,
Then backtrack and a right turn
To the west, across the road and into Kensington Gardens

And out to the chestnut and beech grove
As the dogs go by
                and the Punks noodle along
In their chrome stud belts and Technicolor hair.

What breeze-bristled citics the trees are,
Their lights snatched off and on,
                        streets cluttered with leaves.
The sky is scrubbed to a delft blue
                in the present tense,
Segueing into gray and a future pearl.

I'm stuck here, unwilling to trace my steps back,
The month running down like a love affair
                inexorably to its close,
Sunday, October 30, Pound's birthday ninety-eight years ago,
Everything lidded with gray, unporridgy clouds now,
Smooth as a slice of tin
                or a flat rock in the street.
Like a bouffant hairdo of steel wool,
The limbs of a leafless chestnut tree are back-combed by the wind.
The English mind, he said, the cold soup of the English mind.
At Pisa it all came back
                in a different light
In the wind-sear and sun-sear of the death cages,
Remembering Christmases in the country, the names
Of dead friends in the Tuscan twilight
                building and disappearing across the sky.
Cold soup, cold soup,
Longwater color of pewter,
                late grass green neon.

—Short Riff for John Keats on His 188th Birthday

Hopkins thought your verse abandoned itself
To an enervating luxury,
                    a life of impressions
In fairyland, life of a dreamer,
And lacking the manly virtues of active thought

Born on All Hallows' Eve, what other early introit
Can one summon,
                    that single, arterial drop of blood
On the clean sheet dispelling for good
                    a subsequent second,
Little black light magnet, imagination's Buddha . . .

                                        (November)
—A Traveler between life and death . . .
Where is that line between sleep and sleep,
That line like a wind over water
Rippling toward shore,
                    appearing and disappearing
In wind-rise and wind-falter—
That line between rain and sleet,
                    between leaf-bronze and leaf-drop—

That line where the river stops and the lake begins,
Where the black blackens
                    and light comes out of the light . . .

Stone circle at Castlerigg,
                    Cumbrian, Paleolithic chancel
Against the November mist and vault,

12

Mouth-mark of the invisible, air become breath
And ecclesiastical smoke . . .

Crows, like strings of black Christmas-tree lights, burn in the bare
   trees,
And silver Y moths—though soon to die—appear at dusk,

The night coming down, a dark snow
Piecemeal and hard across the moors
                  like the ashes of Paradise
3500 years ago,
            Helvellyn and Thirlmere
Sluicing to charcoal down-valley, water and earth

And air all bleared to the same color, an indiscriminate estuary
Shoaling into the landscape, nobody here but me
Unspooling to nothingness,
              line after line after latched, untraceable line . . .

—November pares us like green apples,
                  circling under our skins
In long, unbroken spirals until
We are sweet flesh for the elements
               surprised by the wind's shear
Curling down from the north of Wales
Like Occam's edge to Steeple Aston and Oxfordshire.

"Worst time of the year," he said,
             "leaves everywhere
And fresh cold to shiver your very seeds.
I've burned two piles already, Saturday morning yet"—
This in the Norman churchyard,

13

Gray flake and flame in a hushed mound on Delia Johnson,
                                        God Knows His Own,

Lead lines in the arteries for the first time, magpies
Hustling their double notes
                        steadily, like oars in an oarlock,
Beechwoods and whitehorns, hawthorn and mountain ash
All burning down to bare ricks
Against the dropdraft of cold as winter circles and moves in . . .

—Chelsea Embankment, 5 p.m.: Whistler pastels squished
Down the fluted water, orange,
Tamarind, apricot
                        jade on the slate slip of the river,
Tug-ducks moored at the mudbanks,
Southbank light-string reflections stretched like struck and vibrat-
        ing pipes,
The Thames rung softly
                        cross-river, and always a different note
Under the Albert Bridge, the Chelsea and out through town—
Or star-colored steps that sink
Beneath the sharkskin of the current
                                        down to the corridors
And bone-bossed gallery gates of the end.

—I keep coming back, like a tongue to a broken tooth,
Kensington Church Walk,
                        late afternoon,
Pigeons in bas-relief and frieze on the building's edge—
There is no sickness of spirit like homesickness
When what you are sick for
                        has never been seen or heard

14

In this world, or even remembered
                        except as a smear of bleached light
Opening, closing beyond any alphabet's
Recall to witness and isolate . . .

November's my favorite month,
                        the downside of autumn
And winter in first array, the sky
Constabled now and again
Over Kensington Gardens:
                        north of the Serpentine,
A pale light on the bright side of the dark,
Everything starting to glide and refract,
                        moving just under water . . .

—Today is fire and solution, rack
                        of veins in the ruined trees,
A warm wind from the south and crows like mistletoe in the twist
And tuck of diluvial branches—

Stay out of the way and be conspicuous,
Step back and let your story, like water, go where it will,
Cut down your desires,
                        alone, as you are, on the white heart of the earth.

—The sadness of Sunday train rides in the rain,
Little gardens and back yards
Bellied up to the buffed tracks,
Their wet laundry and broken toys beside TO LET signs,
Crushed Styrofoam cups
                        small pockets of old ice turned out,

The joyless twitter of wheels
and couplings turning and changing,
Whole centers of villages
Scooped out and fenced in for a high-rise or a car park,
Anguish of bitten trees, slow
Bull's-eyes of raindrops in flat, colorless water pools,

And all the south of England
Under the sponge,
nothing in sight but the yellow-slickered rail workers
Standing like patient, exotic birds
On the outskirts of Redhill, or upline from Hayward's Heath,
One on one leg, as though poised for frogs,

The desolate, wax faces
Of young mothers gripping their children from side to side
In the fleshed, electric light,
stunned by
Something they never asked for,
Something like somebody else's life, that they've been given,

Sadness of platforms, black umbrellas
Doleful on benches, half-opened, damp,
Tedious sense
Of expectation, the clouds
Continuing on for days past our destinations . . .

(December)
—Noon like cicada wings,
translucence remembered, half-sheets
Of light over light on the black stones

16

Of the crescent walk and bodices of the rhododendron,
Red eye of the whirring sun—
                              December comes out of the ground
Shedding its skin on the bare trees,
And hovers above the northern sky
Wings like new glass,
                         wings like a thousand miles of new glass—

How sweet to think that Nature is solvency,
                              that something empirically true
Lies just under the dead leaves
That will make us anchorites in the dark
Chambers of some celestial perpetuity—
                              nice to think that,
Given the bleak alternative,
Though it hasn't proved so before,
                              and won't now
No matter what things we scrape aside—
                              God is an abstract noun.

—Flashback: a late September Sunday,
                         the V & A courtyard,
Holly and I at one end,
Bronze Buddha under some falling leaves at the other:
Weightlessness of the world's skin
                              undulating like a balloon
Losing its air around us, down drifting down
Through the faint hiss of eternity
Emptying somewhere else
                         O emptying elsewhere
This afternoon, skin

That recovers me and slides me in like a hand
As I unclench and spread
                    finger by finger inside the Buddha's eye . . .

                                        —*London 1983*

March Journal

—After the Rapture comes, and everyone goes away
Quicker than cream in a cat's mouth,
                              all of them gone
In an endless slipknot down the sky
                              and its pink tongue
Into the black hole of Somewhere Else,

What will we do, left with the empty spaces of our lives
Intact,
        the radio frequencies still unchanged,
The same houses up for sale,
Same books unread,
                    all comfort gone and its comforting . . .

For us, the earth is a turbulent rest,
                              a different bed
Altogether, and kinder than that—
After the first death is the second,
A little fire in the afterglow,
                    somewhere to warm your hands.

—The clean, clear line, incised, unbleeding,
Sharp and declarative as a cut
                    the instant before the blood wells out . . .

—March Blues
The insides were blue, the color of Power Putty,
When Luke dissected the dogfish,
                              a plastic blue
In the whey
              sharkskin infenestrated:
Its severed tailfin bobbed like a wing nut in another pan
As he explained the dye job
                              and what connected with what,
Its pinned lips skewed and pointed straight-lined at the ceiling,
The insides so blue, so blue . . .

March gets its second wind,
                              starlings high shine in the trees
As dread puts its left foot down and then the other.
Buds hold their breaths and sit tight.
The weeping cherries
                    lower their languorous necks and nibble the grass
Sprout ends that jump headfirst from the ground,
Magnolia drums blue weight
                              next door when the sun is right.

—Rhythm comes from the roots of the world,
                              rehearsed and expandable.

—After the ice storm a shower of crystal down from the trees
Shattering over the ground
                              like cut glass twirling its rainbows,
Sunlight in flushed layers under the clouds,
Twirling and disappearing into the clenched March grass.

—Structure is binary, intent on a resolution,
Its parts tight but the whole loose
                              and endlessly repetitious.

—And here we stand, caught
In the crucifixal noon
                              with its bled, attendant bells,
And nothing to answer back with
Forsythia purrs in its burning shell,
Jonquils, like Dante's angels, appear from their blue shoots.

How can we think to know of another's desire for darkness,
· That low coo like a dove's
                              insistent outside the heart's window?
How can we think to think this?
How can we sit here, crossing out line after line,
Such five-finger exercises
                              up and down, learning our scales,

And say that all quartets are eschatological
Heuristically
                    when the willows swim like medusas through the trees,
Their skins beginning to blister into a 1000 green welts?
How can we think to know these things,
Clouds like full suds in the sky
                              keeping away, keeping away?

—Form is finite, an undestroyable hush over all things.

A Journal of True Confessions

—Power rigs drift like lights out past the breakwater,
                                    white, and fluorescent white,
The sea moving them up and down
In the burgeoning dawn,
                        up and down,
White as they drift and flicker over the salmon run,

Engines cut, or cut back,
Trolling herring bait or flasher lures,
                                    the sea moving them up and down,
The day's great hand unfolding
Its palm as the boats drift with the tide's drift:

All morning we slipped among them,
                                    Ray at the boat's wheel
Maneuvering, baiting the double hooks, tying and cutting,
Getting the depth right,
                        Mark and I
Watching the rods as their almost-invisible lines

Trailed through the boat's wake,
                                    waiting for each to dip:
And when it came
We set the drag and played him,
                                    the salmon jumping and silver,
Then settled like quick foil in the net's green . . .

22

Later, ground zero, the Straits of Juan de Fuca
                              sliding the fog out
Uncharacteristically, sunlight letting its lines down
For a last run,
            glint from the water like flecked scales,
Everything easing away, away,

Waves, and the sea-slack, sunset,
Tide's bolt shot and turned for the night,
The dark coming in,
                        dark like the dogfish coming in
Under the island's eyelid, under and down.
                                              —15 July 1984

—Lashed to the syllable and noun,
                        the strict Armageddon of the verb,
I lolled for seventeen years
Above this bay with its antimacassars of foam
On the rocks, the white, triangular tears
                        sailboats poke through the sea's spun sheet,
Houses like wads of paper dropped in the moss clumps of the trees,
Fog in its dress whites at ease along the horizon,
Trying to get the description right.
                              If nothing else,
It showed me that what you see
                        both is and is not there,
The unseen bulking in from the edges of all things,
Changing the frame with its nothingness.

Its blue immensity taught me about subtraction,
Those luminous fingerprints
                        left by the dark, their whorls

23

Locked in the stations of the pilgrim sun.
It taught me to underlook.
Turkey buzzards turn in their widening spins
                                    over the flint
Ridged, flake-dried ground and kelp beds,
Sway-winged and shadowless in the climbing air.
Palm trees postcard the shoreline.
Something is added as the birds disappear,
                                    something quite small
And indistinct and palpable as a stain
                                    of saint light on a choir stall.
                                    —6 August 1984

—I can write a simple, declarative English sentence,
Mancini said,
                drinking a stinger and leaning back
In his green chair above the Arno.
                        And not many can say that,
He added, running the peppermint taste
Around on his tongue.
                Out on the river,
Down below Prato, the sun was lowering its burned body
Into the shadows.
                Happy birthday, Lieutenant,
He quipped, and ordered another round.

Twenty-four years ago, and dog days, indeed, Fortunatus.
Six months later
                (flash-forward across the Aegean),
Tell Laura I Love Her PA'ed the ship's lounge, the Captain's arm
Around my shoulders, full moonlight and Jesus
                                    everything in the sky

Was beautiful ...
                I ducked out and turned back down to 2nd Class,
His sweet invective lotioning my right ear.
And stingers that night as well, for hours out of Piraeus,
Mancini grinning like Ungaretti,
                        And then he said, What?

The stars are fastening their big buckle,
                        and flashy night shoes,
Thunder chases its own tail down the sky,
My forty-ninth year, and all my Southern senses called to horn,
August night hanging like cobwebs around my shoulders:
How existential it all is, really,
                        the starting point always the starting point
And what's-to-come still being the What's-to-Come.
Some friends, like George, lurk in the memory like locusts,
                        while others, flat one-sided fish
Looking up, handle themselves like sweet stuff:
                        look out for them, look out for them.
                        —25 August 1984

—Cicadas wind up their one note to a breaking point.
The sunlight, like fine thread, opens and closes us.
The wind, its voice like grasshoppers' wings,
                        rises and falls.
Sadness is truer than happiness.

Walking tonight through the dwarf orchard,
The fruit trees seem etched like a Dürer woodcut against the sky,
The odd fruit
                burined in bas-relief,

25

The moon with its one foot out of the clouds,
All twenty-one trees growing darker in a deepening dark.

When the right words are found I will take them in and be filled
    through with joy.
My mouth will be precious then,
                           as your mouth is precious.
If you want to hear me, you'll have to listen again,
You'll have to listen to what the wind says,
                        whatever its next direction.
                      —9 *September* 1984

—It's all such a matter of abstracts—
                    love with its mouth wide open,
Affection holding its hand out,
Impalpable to the impalpable—
No one can separate the light from the light.

They say that he comes with clouds,
The faithful witness,
               the first-begotten of the dead.
And his feet are like fine brass,
His voice the perpetual sound of many waters.

The night sky is darker than the world below the world,
The stars medieval cathedral slits from a long way.
This is the dark of the *Metamorphoses*
When sparks from the horses' hooves
                  showed us Persephone
And the Prince's car in its slash and plunge toward Hell.

26

Seventy-four years ago today,

                    Dino Campana, on the way back

From his pilgrimage on foot

To the holy chill of La Verna inside the Apennines

To kiss the rock where St. Francis received the stigmata,

Stopped in a small inn at Monte Filetto

And sat on a balcony all day

                   staring out at the countryside,

The hawks circling like lost angels against the painted paradise of
    the sky,

The slope below him

               a golden painting hung from the walnut tree:

The new line will be like the first line,

                   spacial and self-contained,

Firm to the touch

But intimate, carved, as though whispered into the ear.

                         —25 September 1984

—The dragon maple is shedding its scales and wet sides,

Scuffs of cloud bump past the Blue Ridge

                   looking for home,

Some nowhere that's somewhere for them,

The iris teeter and poke on their clubbed feet:

October settles its whole weight in a blue study.

I think of the great painters in light like this,

                   Morandi's line

Drawn on the unredemptive air, Picasso's cut

Like a laser into the dark hard of the mystery,

Cézanne with his cross-tooth brush and hook,
And sad, immaculate Rothko,
                        whose line was no line at all,

His last light crusted and weighed down,
                            holes within holes,
This canvas filled with an emptiness, this one half full
Like the sky over Locust Avenue. Like the grass.
                                —5 October 1984

—What disappears is what stays . . .
O'Grady stories abound.
                        Born one day later than I was, my alter ego,
He points at me constantly
Across the years
                        from via dei Giubbonari in Rome, spring 1965,
Asking me where the cadence is,
Dolce vitaed and nimbus-haired,
                        where's the measure we talked about?
His finger blurs in my eye.
Outside the picture,
            the Largo looms in the bleached distance behind his back.

I look for it, Desmond, I look for it constantly
In the long, musical shape of the afternoon,
                        in the slice of sunlight pulled
Through the bulge of the ash trees
Opening like a lanced ache in the front yard,
In the sure line the mockingbird takes
                        down from the privet hedge

And over the lawn where the early shade
Puddles like bass chords under the oak,
In the tangent of 4 p.m., in the uncut grass,
            in the tangle and tongue-tie it smooths there . . .

But our lines seem such sad notes for the most part,
Pinned like reliquaries and stopgaps
                        to the cloth effigy of some saint
I laid out in the public niche
Of a mission or monastery—
St. Xavier, hear me,
            St. Xavier, hear my heart,
Give my life meaning, heal me and take me in,
The dust like a golden net from the daylight outside
Over everything,
            candles chewing away at the darkness with their numb teeth.
                                —19 October 1984

—According to Freud, Leonardo da Vinci made up a wax paste
For his walks from which
                        he fashioned delicate animal figurines,
Hollow and filled with air.
When he breathed into them, they floated
Like small balloons, twisting and turning,
                        released by the air
Like Li Po's poems downriver, downwind
To the undergrowth and the sunlight's dissembling balm.
What Freud certainly made of this
Is one thing.
            What does it mean to you,
Amber menagerie swept from his sun-struck and amber hands?

29

Giorgio Vasari told it first,

                and told us this one as well:
A wine grower from Belvedere
Found an uncommon lizard and gave it to Leonardo
Who made wings for it out of the skins
Of other lizards,

                and filled the wings with mercury
Which caused them to wave and quiver
Whenever the lizard moved.

                He made eyes, a beard and two horns
In the same way, tamed it, and kept it in a large box
To terrify his friends.

                His games were the pure games of children,
Asking for nothing but artifice, beauty and fear.

                        —20 October 1984

—Function is form, form function back here where the fruit trees
Strip to November's music,
And the black cat and the tortoiseshell cat

                crouch and slink,
Crouch and slink toward something I can't see
But hear the occasional fateful rustlings of,
Where the last tomatoes seep

                from their red skins through the red dirt,
And sweet woodruff holds up its smooth gray sticks
Like a room full of boys

                all wanting to be excused at the same time:

The song of white lights and power boats,

                the sails of August and late July devolve
To simple description in the end,

Something about a dark suture
Across the lawn,
             something about the way the day snips
It open and closes it
When what-comes-out has come out
                          and burns hard in its vacancy,
Emerging elsewhere restructured and restrung,
Like a tall cloud that all the rain has fallen out of.

The last warm wind of summer
                          shines in the dogwood trees
Across the street, flamingoing berries and cupped leaves
That wait to be cracked like lice
Between winter's fingernails.
                          The season rusts to these odd stains
And melodramatic stutterings
In the bare spots of the yard, in the gutter angles
Brimming with crisp leftovers,
                          and gulled blooms in the rhododendrons,
Veneer, like a hard wax, of nothing on everything.

                          —3 November 1984

Night Journal

—I think of Issa, a man of few words:
The world of dew
Is the world of dew.
And yet . . .
And yet . . .

—Three words contain
                        all that we know for sure of the next life
Or the last one: Close your eyes.
Everything else is gossip,
                        false mirrors, trick windows
Flashing like Dutch glass
In the undiminishable sun.

—I write it down in visible ink,
Black words that disappear when held up to the light—
I write it down
            not to remember but to forget,
Words like thousands of pieces of shot film
                                    exposed to the sun.
I never see anything but the ground.

—Everyone wants to tell his story.
The Chinese say we live in the world of the 10,000 things,
Each of the 10,000 things
                        crying out to us

Precisely nothing,
A silence whose tune we've come to understand,
Words like birthmarks,

        embolic sunsets drying behind the tongue.
If we were as eloquent,
If what we say could spread the good news the way that dogwood
    does,
Its votive candles

        phosphorous and articulate in the green haze
Of spring, surely something would hear us.

—Even a chip of beauty
        is beauty intractable in the mind,
Words the color of wind
Moving across the fields there
        wind-addled and wind-sprung,
Abstracted as water glints,
The fields lion-colored and rope-colored,
As in a picture of Paradise,
        the bodies languishing over the sky
Trailing their dark identities
That drift off and sieve away to the nothingness
Behind them
        moving across the fields there
As words move, slowly, trailing their dark identities.

—Our words, like blown kisses, are swallowed by ghosts
Along the way,
        their destinations bereft
In a rub of brightness unending:
How distant everything always is,
        and yet how close,

Music starting to rise like smoke from under the trees.

—Birds sing an atonal row
                              unsyncopated
From tree to tree,
                    dew chants
Whose songs have no words
                              from tree to tree
When night puts her dark lens in,
One on this limb, two others back there.

—Words, like all things, are caught in their finitude.
They start here, they finish here
No matter how high they rise—
                              my judgment is that I know this
And never love anything hard enough
That would stamp me
                    and sink me suddenly into bliss.

A Journal of the Year of the Ox

—January,
>   the dragon maple sunk in its bones,
The sky gray gouache and impediment.
Pity the poor pilgrim, the setter-forth,
Under a sweep so sure,
>   pity his going up and his going down.

Each year I remember less.
This past year it's been
>   the Long Island of the Holston
And all its keening wires
>   in a west wind that seemed to blow constantly,
Lisping the sins of the Cherokee.

How shall we hold on, when everything bright falls away?
How shall we know what calls us
>   when what's past remains what's past
And unredeemed, the crystal
And wavering coefficient of what's ahead?

Thursday, purgatorial Thursday,
The Blue Ridge etched in smoke
>   through the leaded panes of the oak trees,
There, then not there,
A lone squirrel running the power line,
>   neck bowed like a tiny buffalo:

The Long Island of the Holston,
                    sacred refuge ground
Of the Cherokee Nation:
              nothing was ever killed there.
I used to cross it twice whenever I drove to the golf course.
Nobody tells you anything.

The ghost of Dragging Canoe
              settles like snowflakes on the limbs
Of the river bushes, a cold, white drift
That bleeds when it breaks.
              Everyone wants to touch its hem
Now that it's fallen, everyone wants to see its face.

———————

What sifts us down through a blade-change
              stays hidden from us,
But sifts us the same,
Scores us and alters us utterly:
From somewhere inside and somewhere outside, it smooths us
    down.

———————

Here's your Spook, Indaco said,
              sliding the imitation Sandeman's sherry figurine
Toward me along the bar, memento
And laughingstock of the 163rd,
              stamped out by the thousands
At Nove, two hours up the road.

It's usually a ceremony, all your colleagues
And fellow officers standing absurdly about

Happy you're leaving, and you too,
                                    everyone half drunk
And hilarious in his cordovan shoes.

But not this time, Indaco wadding the paper sack up,
He and someone whose name I can't call back
                        letting me go for good, and glad of it:
I'd lost one document, I wore my hair long, I burned it by accident
And no one ever forgot

Such small failures, such sleeveless oblivions
We passed through
                        trying to get our lives to fit right
In what was available from day to day,
And art,
            and then the obvious end of art, that grace

Beyond its reach
                    I'd see each night as I thumbed the Berensons
And argued with Hobart and Schneeman
                                        that what's outside
The picture is more important than what's in.
They didn't agree any more than Indaco had,

All of us hungering after righteousness
Like Paul Cézanne, we thought, in his constancy.
Or Aeneas with the golden bough
                        sweeping through Hell.
O we were luminous in our ignorance O we were true.

———————

Form comes from form, it's said:
                    nothing is ever ended,

39

A spilling like shook glass in the air,
Water over water,
        flame out of flame,
Whatever we can't see, whatever we can't touch,
            unfixed and shining . . .

And today I remember nothing.
The sky is a wrung-out, China blue
        and hides no meanings.
The trees have a pewter tinge and hide no meanings.
All of it hustles over me like a wind
        and reminds me of nothing.

Nobody rises out of the ground in a gold mist.
Nobody slides like an acrobat
        out of the endless atmosphere.
Nobody touches my face
Or hand.
      Not a word is said that reminds me of anything

And O it is cold now by the fake Etruscan urn
And six miniature box bushes
        nobody stands beside
In the real wind tightening its scarf
Around the white throats
        of everyone who is not here.

The cold, almost solid, lies
Like snow outside
        in the tufted spikes of the seed grass

And footprints we didn't leave
That cross the driveway and disappear up the front steps.

It's not the darkness we die of, as someone said,
                              seamless and shut tight
As water we warm up and rock in,
But cold, the cold with its quartz teeth
And fingernails
             that wears us away, wears us away

Into an afterthought.
                  Or a glint
Down there by the dwarf spruce and the squirrel run.
Or one of the absences who lips at the edge of understanding
Wherever I turn,
             as pursed and glittering as a kiss.
                              —20 January 1985

—The sunset, Mannerist clouds
                  just shy of the Blue Ridge
Gainsay the age before they lose their blush
In the rising coagulation of five o'clock.
Two dark, unidentifiable birds
                  swoop and climb
Out of the picture, the white-slatted, red-roofed Munch house
Gathering light as the evening begins to clot.
The trees dissolve in their plenitude
                  into a dark forest
And streetlights come on to stare like praying mantises down on us.

Next morning all's inside out,
                  the winter trees with their nervous systems

Snatched up and sparkless against the sky.
Light lies without desire on the black wires
And the white wires,
                    the dead leaves sing like gnats,
Rising and settling back when the wind comes.
How does one deal with what is always falling away,
Returning diminished with each turn?
The grass knows, drummed in its lockjaw bed,

                                   but it won't tell.
                                   —30 January 1985

—We stand at the green gates,
                              substitutes for the unseen
Rising like water inside our bodies,
Stand-ins against the invisible:
It's the blank sky of the page
                    —not the words it's never the words—
That backgrounds our lives:
It's you always you and not your new suit
That elicits solicitude:
The unknown repeats us, and quickens our in-between.

Winter is like that—abstract,
                              flat planes and slashes,
The Blue Ridge like a worm's back
Straight ahead,
                    one skewed hump and then a smooth one,
Hallelujah of tree branches and telephone poles
In front, and a house or two and a nurse:
February music,
                    high notes and a thin line strung
For us to cleave to, black notes

Someone is humming we haven't been introduced to:
Like the stone inside a rock,
                    the stillness of form is the center of everything,
Inalterable, always at ease.

                              —7 February 1985

—The rain, in its white disguise,

                              has nothing to say to the wind
That carries it, whose shoulders
It stops from giving no signal, aimlessly, one drop
At a time, no word
Or gesture to what has carried it all this way for nothing.

This is the disappearance we all dreamed of when young,
Without apology, tougher than water, no word
To anyone,
            disguised as ourselves
And unrecognizable, unique
And indistinguishable from what we disappeared into.

                              —13 February 1985

—One, one and by one we all slip into the landscape,
Under the muddy patches,
                    locked in the frozen bud
Of the down-leafed rhododendron,
Or blurred in the echoing white of a rabbit's tail
Chalked on the winter's dark
                    in the back yard or the driveway.

One, one and by one we all sift to a difference
And cry out if one of our branches snaps
                              or our bark is cut.

43

The winter sunlight scours us,
The winter wind is our comfort and consolation.
We settle into our ruin

One, one and by one as we slip from clear rags into feathery skin
Or juice-in-the-ground, pooled
And biding its time
                         backwashed under the click peach tree
One, one and by one thrust up by the creek bank,
Huddled in spongy colonies,
                              longing to be listened to.

Here I am, here I am, we all say,
                        I'm back,
Rustle and wave, chatter and spring
Up to the air, the sweet air.
Hardened around the woodpecker's hole, under his down,
We all slip into the landscape, one, one and by one.
                            —25 February 1985

—Fever and ooze, fever and ooze:
Pronoun by pronoun, verb by irregular verb,
Winter grows great with spring: March:
                              already something has let loose
Deep in the hidden undersprings
Of the year, looking for some way out: moss sings
At the threshold, tongues wag
                        down the secret valleys and dark draws
Under the sun-stunned grass:
What can't stop comes on, mewling like blood-rush in the ear,

Balancing over the sunken world:

> fever and ooze, fever and ooze.

> —9 *March* 1985

—I used to sit on one of the benches along the Adige
In a small park up-river from S. Anastasia

> from time to time

When I lived in Verona,

> the Roman theater like lapped wings

On some seabird across the water
Unable to rise, half folded, half turned in the pocked air
The river spray threw up

> on me and on it.

Catullus's seat—VALERI—was carved on top of the left-hand wing.
I used to try to imagine—delicious impossibility—
What it must have been like to be him,

> his vowels and consonants

The color of bee wings hived in the bee-colored afternoons.
An iron-spiked and barbed-wire jut-out and overhang loomed
Just to my left.

> I always sat as close to it as I could.

I remember a woman I saw there once,

> in March,

The daylight starting to shake its hair out like torch flames
Across the river,

> the season poised like a veiled bride,

White foot in its golden shoe
Beating the ground, full of desire, white foot at the white
  threshold.

She stared at the conched hillside
                    as though the season became her,
As though a threshold were opening
Somewhere inside her, no woman more beautiful than she was,
No song more insistent than the beat of that white foot,
As she stepped over,
                    full of desire,
Her golden shoe like a sun in the day's deep chamber.
I remember the way she looked as she stood there,
                         That look on her face.
                         —27 March 1985

—Such a hustle of blue skies from the west,
                         the pre-Columbian clouds
Brooding and looking straight down,
The white plumes of the crab-apple tree
Plunging and streaming in their invisible headgear.

April plugs in the rosebud
                    and its Tiffany limbs.
This earth is a plenitude, but it all twists into the dark,
The not no image can cut
Or color replenish.
                    Not red, not yellow, not blue.
                         —9 April 1985

—Draining the Great Valley of Southwest Virginia
                         and Upper East Tennessee,
The Holston River cuts through the water gaps and the wind gaps
In the Stone Mountains and Iron Mountains
Northeast-southwest,
                    a trellis pattern of feeder streams

Like a grid from Saltville in the north
To Morristown and Jefferson City in the south
Overlaying the uplifts and folds
                                    and crystalline highlands
That define and channel the main valley,
Clinch Mountain forming a western wall,
The Great Smokies and the Unakas dominant in the south.

In 1779 it took John Donelson from December till March
To go from Kingsport to Knoxville on it
By flatboat, a distance nowadays of two hours by car.
All of my childhood was spent on rivers,
The Tennessee and Hiwassee, the Little Pigeon,
The Watauga and Holston.
                            There's something about a river
No ocean can answer to:
Leonardo da Vinci,
                in one of his notebooks,
Says that the water you touch is the last of what has passed by
And the first of what's to come.

The Cherokee called it Hogoheegee,
                            the Holston,
From its source in Virginia down to the mouth of the French
    Broad.
Donelson's flotilla to Middle Tennessee
From Fort Patrick Henry
                            —one of the singular achievements
In opening the West—
Began from the Long Island of the Holston, across
The river and upwind of the fort.
It took them four months, down the Holston and Tennessee,

Up the Ohio and Cumberland,
                              to reach Nashville,
The Big Salt Lick, and the log cabins of settlement.

Intended by God's Permission, his journal said,
Through Indian ambush, death by drowning, death by fire,
Privation and frostbite,
                              their clothes much cut by bullets,
Over the thirty miles of Muscle Shoals,
Loss of the pox-carrying boat and its twenty-eight people
Which followed behind in quarantine and was cut off,
Intercepted, and all its occupants
                              butchered or taken prisoner
Their cries distinctly heard by those boats in the rear,
Passage beyond the Whirl,
                              the suckpool by Cumberland Mountain,
Slaughter of swans, slaughter of buffalo,
                              Intended by God's Permission . . .

Imagine them standing there
                              in full headdress and harness
Having to give it all up,
                              another agreement in blackface,
This one the Long Island of the Holston Peace Treaty,
Ending, the first time, the Cherokee Nation.
Imagine them standing very still,
Protecting their families, hoping to hang on to their one life.
Imagine the way they must have felt
                              agreeing to give away
What wasn't assignable,
The ground that everyone walked on,
                              all the magic of water,

48

Wind in the trees, sunlight, all the magic of water.

—*16 April 1985*

—April, and mirror-slide of the fatal quiet,
Butterflies in a dark confusion over the flower's clenched cheeks,
The smell of chlorophyll

climbing like desperation across my skin:
The maple is flecked, and the sky is choked with cloud tufts
That print a bluek alphabet

along the hillsides and short lawns,
Block gutturals and half thoughts
Against the oily valves opening and closing in the leaves,
Edgy, autumnal morning,
April, stretched out at ease above the garden,

that rises and bows
To whatever it fancies:
Precious stones, the wind's cloth, Prester John or the boy-king of
Babylon,
April,
dank, unseasonable winter of the dead.

—*27 April 1985*

—*Visiting Emily Dickinson*

We stood in the cupola for a while,

JT, Joe Langland and I,
And then they left and I sat
Where she'd sat, and looked through the oak tree toward the hat
factory
And down to the river, the railroad

Still there, the streets where the caissons growled

with their blue meat

49

Still there, and Austin and Sue's still there
Next door on the other side.
And the train station at the top of the hill.
                              And I sat there and I sat there

A decade or so ago
One afternoon toward the end of winter, the oak tree
Floating its ganglia like a dark cloud
                              outside the window.
Or like a medusa hung up to dry.

And nothing came up through my feet like electric fire.
And no one appeared in a white dress
                              with white flowers
Clutched in her white, tiny hands:
No voice from nowhere said anything
                              about living and dying in 1862.

But I liked it there. I liked
The way sunlight lay like a shirtwaist over the window seat.
I liked the view down to the garden.
                              I liked the boxwood and evergreens
And the wren-like, sherry-eyed figure

I kept thinking I saw there
                              as the skies started to blossom
And a noiseless noise began to come from the orchard—
And I sat very still, and listened hard
And thought I heard it again.
                              And then there was nothing, nothing at all,

The slick bodice of sunlight
                              smoothed out on the floorboards,

The crystal I'd turned inside of

Dissembling to shine and a glaze somewhere near the window-
    panes,

Voices starting to drift up from downstairs,

                              somebody calling my name . . .

                                      —6 May 1985

—Ficino tells us the Absolute

Wakens the drowsy, lights the obscure,

                              revives the dead,

Gives form to the formless and finishes the incomplete.

What better good can be spoken of?

                              —9 May 1985

—In the first inch of afternoon, under the peach trees,

The constellations of sunlight

Sifting along their courses among the posed limbs,

It's hard to imagine the north wind

                            wishing us ill,

Revealing nothing at all and wishing us ill

In God's third face.

                The world is an ampersand,

And I lie in sweet clover,

                      bees like golden earrings

Dangling and locked fast to its white heads,

Watching the clouds move and the constellations of light move

Through the trees, as they both will

When the wind weathers them on their way,

When the wind weathers them to that point

                        where all things meet.

                       —15 May 1985

—For two months I've wanted to write about Edgar Allan Poe
Who lived for a year where I live now
In 1826,
       the year that Mr. Jefferson died.
He lived, appropriately enough, at 13 West Range:
One room with a fireplace and bed,
               one table and candlestick,
A small trunk and a washstand.
There's a top hat and a black hat box on the trunk lid
The ruffled gray cape on the clothes rack
                and a bowl of mold-haired fruit
On the washstand.
       There's a mirror and cane-back chair.

Over the door, in Latin, are bronze words
About the *Magni Poetae* which I don't believe
Any more now than I used to before I lived here.
Still, there's something about the place
               that draws me
A couple of times a week
To peer through the slab-glass door,
To knock twice with my left hand on the left doorjamb
Each time I go there,
        hoping to call the spirits up
Or just to say hello.
       He died in fear and away from home.

I went to his grave once in Baltimore,
           a young lieutenant
Intent on intensity.
I can't remember what I thought it meant to me then,
But can remember going back to the BOQ

To sit up most of the night

                drinking red wine and reading a book of poems.
Here in Virginia when I visit his room and knock
Twice on the doorjamb, and look at the rump-sprung mattress,
The spirits come and my skin sings.
I still don't know why

           but I think it's all right, and I like it.

                    —23 *May* 1985

—Horn music starts up and stutters uncertainly

                out of the brown house
Across the street: a solo,
A duet, then three of them all at once, then silence,
Then up and back down the scale.
Sunday, the ninth of June, the morning
Still dull-eyed in its green kimono,

            the loose, blown sleeves
Moving complacently in the wind.
Now there are two, then all three again

           weaving a blurred, harmonic line
Through the oak trees and the dogwood
As the wind blows and the sheer nightgown of daylight glints.

Where was it I heard before
Those same runs and half-riffs

           turned through a summer morning,
Come from one of the pastel buildings
Outside the window I sat in front of looking down
As I tried to practice my own scales

           of invisible music
I thought I heard for hours on a yellow legal pad?
Verona, I think, the stiff French horn

Each weekend echoing my own false notes
                                    and scrambled lines
I tried to use as decoys to coax the real things down
Out of the air they hid in and out of the pencils they hid in . . .

Silence again. For good, now,
I suspect, until next week,
                              arduous harmony,
Unalterable music our lives are measured by.
What will become of us, the Italian French horn player,
These players, me, all of us
                              trying to imitate
What we can't see and what we can't hear?
Nothing spectacular, I would guess, a life
Scored more or less by others,
                              smorzando here, *andante* there:
Only the music will stay untouched,
Moving as certainly as the wind moves,
                                    invisible in the trees.
                                    —*12 June 1985*

—North wind flows from the mountain like water,
                                    a clear constancy
Runneling through the grapevines,
Slipping and eddying over the furrows the grasses make
Between the heaves and slackening of the vine rows,
Easing and lengthening over the trees,
                                    then smooth, flat
And without sound onto the plain below.
It parts the lizard-colored beech leaves,
Nudges and slithers around
                              the winter-killed cypress

Which stand like odd animals,
Brown-furred and hung from the sky,
                        backwashes against the hillsides
And nibbles my cheeks and hands
Where I stand on the balcony letting it scour me.
Lamentation of finches,
                harangue of the sparrow,
Nothing else moves but wind in the dog-sleep of late afternoon . . .

Inside the self is another self like a black hole
Constantly dying, pulling parts of our lives
Always into its fluttery light,
                        anxious as Augustine
For redemption and explanation:
No birds hang in its painted and polished skies, no trees
Mark and exclaim its hill lines,
                no grass moves, no water:

Like souls looking for bodies after some Last Judgment,
Forgotten incidents rise
                from under the stone slabs
Into its waxed air;
Grief sits like a toad with its cheeks puffed,
Immovable, motionless, its tongue like a trick whip
Picking our sorrows off, our days and our happiness;

Despair, with its three mouths full,
Dangles our good occasions, such as they are, in its gray hands,
Feeding them in,
                medieval and naked in their ecstasy;

55

And Death, a tiny o of blackness,
Waits like an eye for us to fall through its retina,
A minor irritation,
          so it can blink us back.

———————

Nothing's so beautiful as the memory of it
Gathering light as glass does,
As glass does when the sundown is on it
          And darkness is still a thousand miles away.

———————

Last night, in the second yard, salmon-smoke in the west
Back-vaulting the bats
          who plunged and swooped like wrong angels
Hooking their slipped souls in the twilight,
The quattrocento landscape
          turning to air beneath my feet,
I sat on the stone wall as the white shirts of my son and friend
Moved through the upper yard like candles
Among the fruit trees,
          and the high voices of children
Sifted like mist from the road below
In a game I'd never played,
          and knew that everything was a shining,
That whatever I could see was filled with the drained light
Lapping away from me quietly,
Disappearing between the vine rows,
          creeping back through the hills,
That anything I could feel,
          anything I could put my hand on—

The damasked mimosa leaf,
The stone ball on the gate post, the snail shell in its still turning—
Would burst into brilliance at my touch.
But I sat still, and I touched nothing,
                              afraid that something might change
And change me beyond my knowing,
That everything I had hoped for, all I had ever wanted,
Might actually happen,
                              So I sat still and touched nothing.

———————

6:30, summer evening, the swallow's hour
Over the vine rows:
                    arrowing down the valley, banking back
And sliding against the wind, they feint
And rise, invisible sustenance disappearing
Out of the air:
                    in the long, dark beams of the farmhouse,
The termites and rhinocerous beetles bore in their slow lines
Under another sky:
                    everything eats or is eaten.

———————

I find myself in my own image, and am neither and both.
I come and go in myself
                    as though from room to room,
As though the smooth incarnation of some medieval spirit
Escaping my own mouth and reswallowed at leisure,
Dissembling and at my ease.
The dove drones on the hillside,
                    hidden inside the dead pine tree.

The wasp drills through the air.
I am neither, I am both.
Inside the turtle dove is the turtle dove,
                              a serious moan.
Inside the wasp we don't know, and a single drop of poison.

———————

This part of the farmhouse was built in the fourteenth century.
Huge chains hold the central beam
                         and the wall together
It creaks like a ship when the walls shift in the afternoon wind.

———————

Who is it here in the night garden,
                              gown a transparent rose
Down to his ankles, great sleeves
Spreading the darkness around him wherever he steps,
Laurel corona encircling his red transparent headcap,
Pointing toward the Madonna?
Who else could it be,
                    voice like a slow rip through silk cloth
In disapproval? *Brother*, he says, pointing insistently,
A sound of voices starting to turn in the wind and then disappear
    as though
Orbiting us, *Brother, remember the way it was*
In my time: nothing has changed:
Penitents terrace the mountainside, the stars hang in their bright
    courses
And darkness is still the dark:
                         concentrate, listen hard,
Look to the nature of all things,

And vanished into the oncoming disappearing
Circle of voices slipstreaming through the oiled evening.

Hmmm . . . Not exactly transplendent:
                    Look to the nature of all things . . .
The clouds slide from the west to the east
Over the Berici Mountains, hiding the half of what he spoke of.
Wind is asleep in the trees,
                    weighing the shelled leaves down.
A radio comes and goes from a parked car below the hill.
What *is* it these children chant about
In their games?
                    Why are their voices so like those
I thought I heard just moments ago
Centrifugal in their extantsy?
                    Concentrate, listen hard . . .
A motor scooter whines up the hill road, toward the Madonna.
                            —9 July 1985
                            (*Cà Paruta*)

—All morning the long-bellied, two-hitched drag trucks
Have ground down the mountainside
                    loaded with huge, cut stone
From two quarries being worked
Some miles up the slope. Rock-drilled and squared-off,
They make the brakes sing and the tires moan,
A music of sure contrition that troubles our ears
And shudders the farmhouse walls.
                    No one around here seems to know
Where the great loads go or what they are being used for.
But everyone suffers the music,

We all sway to the same tune
                    when the great stones pass by,
A weight that keeps us pressed to our chairs
And pushes our heads down, and slows our feet.

———————

Volcanic originally, the Euganean hills
Make up a tiny part,
                    upper northeast, of the Po flood plain
Monasteries and radar stations
Relay the word from their isolate concentration,
Grouped, as they are, like bread mold
                    and terraced like Purgatory.
Their vineyards are visible for miles,
                    cut like a gentle and green
Strip-mining curl up the steep slopes.
During the storm-sweeps out of the Alps,
From a wide distance they stand like a delicate Chinese screen
Against the immensity of the rain.

———————

Outside my door, a cicada turns its engine on.
Above me the radar tower
Tunes its invisible music in:
                    other urgencies tell their stories
Constantly in their sleep,
Other messages plague our ears
                    under Madonna's tongue:
The twilight twists like a screw deeper into the west.

———————

Through scenes of everyday life,
Through the dark allegory of the soul
                                        into the white light of eternity,
The goddess burns in her golden car
From month to month, season to season
                                        high on the walls
At the south edge of Ferrara,
Her votive and reliquary hands
Suspended and settled upon as though under glass,
Offering, giving a gentle benediction:
Reality, symbol and ideal
                                tripartite and everlasting
Under the bricked, Emilian sun.

Borso, the mad uncle, giving a coin to the jester Scoccola,
Borso receiving dignitaries,
                                or out hawking,
Or listening to supplications from someone down on his knees,
Or giving someone his due.
Borso d'Este, Duke of Ferrara and Modena, on a spring day
On horseback off to the hunt:
                                        a dog noses a duck up from a pond,
Peasants are pruning the vines back, and grafting new ones
Delicately, as though in a dance,
Ghostly noblemen ride their horses over the archway,
A child is eating something down to the right,
                                a monkey climbs someone's leg . . .

Such a narrow, meaningful strip
                                of arrows and snakes.
Circles and purple robes, griffins and questing pilgrims:

At the tip of the lion's tail, a courtier rips
A haunch of venison with his teeth;
At the lion's head,
                        someone sits in a brushed, celestial tree.
What darkness can be objectified by this dance pose
And musician holding a dead bird
At each end of the scales?
                        What dark prayer can possibly escape
The black, cracked lips of this mendicant woman on her pooled
        knees?
The shadowy ribbon offers its warnings up
                        under the green eyes of heaven.

Up there, in the third realm,
                        light as though under water
Washes and folds and breaks in small waves
Over each month like sunrise:
                        triumph after triumph
Of pure Abstraction and pure Word, a paradise of white cloth
And white reflections of cloth cross-currented over the cars
With golden wheels and gold leads,
                        all Concept and finery:
Love with her long hair and swans in trace,
Cybele among the Corybants,
Apollo, Medusa's blood and Attis in expiation:
All caught in the tide of light,
                        all burned on the same air.

Is this the progression of our lives,
                        or merely a comment on them?
Is this both the picture and what's outside the picture,

Or decoration opposing boredom
For court ladies to glance up at,
                    crossing a tiled floor?
How much of what we leave do we mean to leave
And how much began as fantasy?
Questions against an idle hour as Borso looks to his hounds.
Virgo reclines on her hard bed
                    under the dragon's heel,
And turreting over the green hills
And the sea, color of sunrise,
                    the city floats in its marbled tear of light.

From my balcony, the intense blue of the under-heaven,
Sapphiric and anodyne,
                    backdrops Madonna's crown.
Later, an arched stretch of cloud,
Like a jet trail or a comet's trail,
                    vaults over it,
A medieval ring of Paradise.
Today, it's that same blue again, blue of redemption
Against which, in the vine rows,
                    the green hugs the ground hard.
Not yet, it seems to say, O not yet.

Heavy Italian afternoon: heat drives like a nail
Through the countryside,
                    everything squirms
Or lies pinned and still in its shining.
On the opposite slope, Alfredo, his long, curved scythe
Flashing and disappearing into the thick junk weeds

63

Between the vine stocks, moves,

                        with a breathy, whooshing sound,
Inexorably as a visitation, or some event
The afternoon's about to become the reoccasion of:
St. Catherine catching the martyr's head

                            in her white hands;
St. Catherine urging the blades on
As the wheel dazzles and turns,
Feeling the first nick like the first rung of Paradise;
St. Catherine climbing, step by step,
The shattering ladder up

                   to the small, bright hurt of the saved.

                            —25 July 1985
                             (Cà Paruta)

—Rilke, di Valmarana, the King of Abyssinia
And countless others once came to wash
At his memory, dipping their hands

                        into the cold waters of his name,
And signing their own
In the vellum, nineteenth-century books
The Commune of Padova provided,

                         each graced page
Now under glass in the fourteenth-century stone rooms
The poet last occupied.
We've come for the same reasons, though the great registers
No longer exist, and no one of such magnitude
Has been in evidence for some years.

                         On the cracked, restored walls,
Atrocious frescoes, like those in an alcove of some trattoria,
Depict the Arcadian pursuits

He often wrote of,
                dotted with puffy likenesses
Of the great man himself, intaglio prints of Laura
And re-creations of famous instances
In his life.
        Poems by devotees are framed and hung up
Strategically here and there.
In short, everything one would hope would not be put forth
In evidence on Petrarch's behalf.

Arquà Petrarca, the town he died in,
                        and this is,
Dangles in folds and cutbacks
Down the mountainside,
                medieval and still undisturbed
In the backwash he retired to, and the zone remains,
Corn, vineyards and fig orchards.
The town's on the other side of the hill, and unseen,
And from the second-floor balcony,
                        southward across the Po Valley,
The prospect is just about
What he would have looked at,
                        the extra roadway and house
Gracious and unobtrusive.
I ghost from room to room and try hard
To reamalgamate everything that stays missing,
To bring together again
                the tapestries and winter fires,
The long walks and solitude
Before the damage of history and an odd fame
Unlayered it all but the one name and a rhyme scheme.

Marconi, Victor Emmanuel II, prince
And princess have come and gone.
                              Outside, in the garden,
The hollyhocks and rose pips move quietly in the late heat.
I write my name in the dirt
                    and knock twice as we leave.

Farfalla comes to my door frame,
                              enters my window,
Swivels and pirouettes, white in the white sunlight,
Farfalla and bumblebee,
Butterfly, wasp and bumblebee
                              together into the dark
Latitudes of my attic, then out
Again, all but la vespa,
The other two into the daylight, a different flower:
Vespa cruises in darkness,
                    checking the corners out,
The charred crevices fit for her habitation, black
Petals for her to light on.

                    ————————

No clouds for four weeks, Madonna stuck
On the blue plate of the sky like sauce
                              left out over night,
Everything flake-red and dust-peppered,
Ants slow on the doorsill,
                    flies languishing on the iron
Railing where no wind jars them.
Dead, stunned heart of summer: the blood stills to a bell pull,

The cry from the watermelon truck

                     hangs like a sheet in the dry air,
The cut grain splinters across the hillside.
All night the stalled dogs bark in our sleep.
All night the rats flutter and roll in the dark loft holes over our
    heads.

———————

An St Augustine tells us, whatever is, is good,
As long as it is,

              even as it rusts and decays
In the paracletic nature of all things:

                     transplendent enough,
I'd say, for our needs, if that's what he meant
Back there in the garden in that circle of voices
Widening out of the sunset and disappearing . . .

———————

Dog fire: quick singes and pops
Of lightning finger the mountainside:

                   the towers and deep dish
Are calling their children in, Madonna is calling her little ones
Out of the sky, such fine flames
To answer to and add up

              as they all come down from the dark.
In the rings and after-chains,
In the great river of language that circles the universe,
Everything comes together,
No word is ever lost,

          no utterance ever abandoned.
They're all borne on the bodiless, glittering currents

That wash us and seek us out:
                              there is a word, one word,
For each of us, circling and holding fast
In all that cascade and light.
Said once, or said twice,
                              it gathers and waits its time to come back
To its true work:
                    concentrate, listen hard.

———

Enormous shadows settle across the countryside,
Scattered and misbegotten.
Clouds slide from the Dolomites
                              as though let out to dry.
Sunset again: that same color of rose leaf and rose water.
The lights of another town
                    tattoo their promises
Soundlessly over the plain.
I'm back in the night garden,
                    the lower yard, between
The three dead fig trees,
Under the skeletal comb-leaves of the fanned mimosa branch,
Gazing at the Madonna,
The swallows and bats at their night work
And I at mine.
                    No scooters or trucks,
No voices of children, no alphabet in the wind:
Only this silence, the strict gospel of silence,
                                        to greet me,
Opened before me like a rare book.
I turn the first page
                    and then the next, but understand nothing,

The deepening twilight a vast vocabulary
I've never heard of.
I keep on turning, however:

                somewhere in here, I know, is my word.
                     —3 *August 1985*
                      (*Cà Paruta*)

—A day licked entirely clean, the landscape resettled
Immeasurably closer, focused
And held still under the ground lens of heaven,

                      the air
As brittle as spun glass:
One of those days the sunlight stays an inch above,

                      or an inch inside
Whatever its tongue touches:
I can't remember my own youth,
That seam of red silt I try so anxiously to unearth:
A handful of dust is a handful of dust,

                      no matter who holds it.
Always the adverb, always the ex-Etcetera . . .

                      20 *August 1985*

—On my fiftieth birthday I awoke
In a Holiday Inn just east of Winchester, Virginia,
The companionable summer rain

                      stitching the countryside
Like bagworms inside its slick cocoon:
The memory of tomorrow is yesterday's storyline:
I ate breakfast and headed south,

                      the Shenandoah
Zigzagging in its small faith
Under the Lee Highway and Interstate 81,

69

First on my left side, then on my right,
Sluggish and underfed,
                            the absences in the heart
Silent as sparrows in the spinning rain:

How do I want to say this?
                            My mother's mother's family
For generations has sifted down
This valley like rain out of Clarke County,
                            seeping into the red clay
Overnight and vanishing into the undergrowth
Of different lives as hard as they could.
Yesterday all of us went
                            to all of the places all of them left from
One way or another,
                            apple groves, scrub oak, gravestones
With short, unmellifluous, unfamiliar names,
Cold wind out of the Blue Ridge,
And reason enough in the lowering sky for leaving
A weight so sure and so fixed . . .

And now it's my turn, same river, same hard-rock landscape
Shifting to past behind me.
                            What makes us leave what we love best?
What is it inside us that keeps erasing itself
When we need it most,
That sends us into uncertainty for its own sake
And holds us flush there
                            until we begin to love it
And have to begin again?
What is it within our own lives we decline to live

Whenever we find it,
                    making our days unendurable,
And nights almost visionless?
I still don't know yet, but I do it.

In my fiftieth year, with a bad back and a worried mind,
Going down the Lee Highway,
                    the farms and villages
Rising like fog behind me,
Between the dream and the disappearance the abiding earth
Affords us each for an instant.
                    However we choose to use it
We use it and then it's gone:
Like the glint of the Shenandoah
                    at Castleman's Ferry,
Like license plates on cars we follow and then pass by,
Like what we hold and let go,
Like this country we've all come down,
                    and where it's led us,
Like what we forgot to say, each time we forget it.
                    25–29 *August 1985*

—Ashes know what burns,
                    clouds savvy which way the wind blows . . .
Full moon like a bed of coals
As autumn revs up and cuts off:
Remembering winter nights like a doused light bulb
Leaning against my skin,
                    object melting into the image
Under the quickly descending stars:
Once the impasse is solved, St. Augustine says, between matter and
    spirit,

71

Evil is merely the absence of good:
Which makes sense, if you understand what it truly means,
Full moon the color of sand now,

                              and still unretractable . . .

In a bad way,
                     I don't even know what I don't know,
Time like a one-eyed jack
                              whose other face I can't see
Hustling me on O hustling me on,
Dark of the moon, far side of the sun, the back half of the sky.
Time is memory, he adds:
It's all in the mind's eye,
                              where everything comes to one,
Conjecture, pure spirit, the evil that matter cannot present us—
As the sentence hides in the ink,
                              as cancer hides in the smoke,
As dark hides in the light,
Time hides in our pockets, not stirring, not weighing much.
                              —5 September 1985

—Still, they tried it again, one last time,
In 1776, the Battle of Island Flats
Outside Fort Patrick Henry
                              on the Long Island of the Holston,
Dragging Canoe and Abraham
                              advancing quicker than frost
With their sworn braves through the countryside.

After a small skirmish between scouts and advance guards,
Dragging Canoe brought three hundred men
Into position along a quarter of a mile

Fortified line of calm frontiersmen
and ended for all time
The Cherokee's mystic Nation
with streams of blood every way.

Never so much execution in so short a time
On the frontier.
Our spies really deserve the greatest applause,
We took a great deal of plunder and many guns.
We have a great reason to believe
They are pouring in greatest numbers upon us
and beg assistance of our friends.

Exaggeration and rhetoric:
Nothing was pouring on them, of course,
but history and its disaffection,
Stripping the vacuum of the Cherokee:
The Battle of Island Flats
Starts the inevitable exodus,
Tsali and the Trail of Tears . . .
—15 September 1985

—Attention is the natural prayer of the soul . . .

September, the bed we lie in between summer and autumn,
Sunday in all the windows,
the slow snow of daylight
Flaking the holly tree and the hedge panes
As it disappears in the odd milk teeth
The grass has bared, both lips back
in the cool suck of dusk.

Prayer wheels, ugly as ice, turn in our eyes:
                              verbs white, nouns white,
Adjectives white on white,
                    they turn in our eyes:
Nothing is lost in my eyes in your eyes
                              nothing is lost
As the wheels whittle and spin,
                    conjunction and adverb
White in the white sky of our eyes,
                              ribbons luffing goodbye . . .

September butterflies, heavy with pollen, leaf down
In ones and pairs from the oak trees
                              through the dwarf orchard
And climb the gold-dusted staves of sunlight toward the south
Like notes from a lush music
                    we always almost hear
But don't quite, and stutter into the understory next door.

Night now. Silence. The flowers redeem
Nothing the season can offer up,
                    stars beginning to chink fast
Overhead, west wind
Shuffling the decks of the orchard leaves.
Silence again,
          a fine ash, a night inside the night.
                              —29 September 1985

—The shadows of leaves on the driveway and just-cut grass,
Blurred and enlarged,
                    riffle in short takes
As though stirred under water, a snicked breeze

Moving their makers cross-current and cross-grained across the pool
The daylight makes in the ash tree
                         and the troubled oak.

These monochromatic early days of October
Throb like a headache just back of the eyes,
                                        a music
Of dull, identical syllables
Almost all vowels,
                    ooohing and aaahing
As though they would break out in speech and tell us something.

But nothing's to be revealed,
It seems:
          each day the shadows blur and enlarge, the rain comes
              and comes back,
A dripping of consonants,
As though it too wanted to tell us something, something
Unlike the shadows and their stray signs,

Unlike the syllable the days make
Behind the eyes, cross-current and cross-grained, and unlike
The sibilance of oak tree and ash.
                         What it wants to tell us
Is ecstasy and always,
Guttural words that hang like bats in the throat,
                              their wings closed, their eyes shut:

What it wants to tell us is damped down, slick with desire,
And unaccountable
                  to weather and its apostrophes,

Dark, sweet dark, and close to hand:
Inside its body, high on a branch, a bird
                              repeats the letters of its secret name
To everything, and everything listens hard.

                              —*4 October 1985*

—Truth is the absence of falsehood,
                              beauty the absence of ugliness,
Jay like a stuffed toy in the pear tree,
Afternoon light aluminum deep on right
                              diluting to aftermath on the lawn,
Jay immobile and fluffed up,
Cloud like a bass note, held and slow, now on the sunlight.
The disillusioned and twice-lapsed, the fallen-away,
Become my constituency:
                              those who would die back
To splendor and rise again
From hurt and unwillingness,
                              their own ash on their tongues,
Are those I would be among,
The called, the bruised by God, by their old ways forsaken
And startled on, the shorn and weakened.

There is no loneliness where the body is.
There is no Pyrrhic degeneration of the soul there,
Dragon maple like sunset,
                              scales fired in the noon's glare
Flaking and twisting when the wind spurts,
Sky-back a Cherokee blue,
                              scales winking and flashing.
The poem is written on glass

I look through to calibrate
                    the azimuth of sun and Blue Ridge,
Angle of rise and fall the season reconstitutes.
My name is written on glass,
The emptiness that form takes, the form of emptiness
The body can never signify,
                    yellow of ash leaves on the grass,
Three birds on the dead oak limb.
                              The heart is a spondee.
                                        —12 October 1985

—It is as though, sitting out here in the dwarf orchard,
The soul had come to rest at the edge of the body,
A vacancy, a small ache,
                    the soul had come to rest
After a long passage over the wasteland and damp season.
It is as though a tree had been taken out of the landscape.
It is as though a tree had been taken out
                              and moved to one side
And the wind blew where the tree had been
As though it had never blown there before,
                                        or that hard.

Tomorrow the rain will come with its lucid elastic threads
Binding the earth and sky.
                    Tomorrow the rain will come
And the soul will start to move again,
Retracing its passage, marking itself
                              back to the center of things.
But today, in the blanched warmth of Indian summer,
It nudges the edge of the body,

The chill luminance of its absence
                                      pulsing and deep,
Extraction the landscape illuminates in the body's night.
                                      —22 October 1985

—The season steps up,
                              repeating its catechism inside the leaves
The dogwoods spell out their beads,
Wind zithers a *Kyrie eleison* over the power lines:
Sunday, humped up in majesty,
                              the new trench for the gas main
Thrums like a healing scar
Across the street, rock-and-roll
Wah-wahs from off the roof next door to Sylvia's house
                              just down the block:

The days peel back, maples kick in their afterburners,
We harry our sins
                    and expiations around the purgatorial strip
We're subject to, eyes sewn shut,
Rocks on our backs,
                    escaping smoke or rising out of the flame,
Hoping the angel's sword
                    unsullied our ashed foreheads,
Hoping the way up is not the way down,
Autumn firestorm in the trees,
                    autumn under our feet . . .
                    —29 October 1985

—I have no interest in anything
                    but the color of leaves,

78

Yellow leaves drawing the light around them
Against the mumped clouds of an early November dusk—
They draw the light like gold foil
                                            around their stiff bodies
And hang like Byzantium in the Byzantine sky.

I have no interest in anything
                                            but the color of blood,
Blood black as a prayer book, flushed from my own body,
China black, lapping the porcelain:
                                            somewhere inside me blood
Is drawing the darkness in,
Stipple by stipple into the darker waters beneath the self.

I have no interest in anything
                                            but the color of breath,
Green as the meat-haunted hum of flies,
Viridian exocrine,
                                            wisp of the wave-urge, jade
Calvary of the begotten sigh,
Alpha of everything, green needle and green syringe.
                                            —11 November 1985

—"If you licked my heart, you'd die,
                                            poisoned by gall and anxiousness."
I read that last night in my first dream.

In the next, the leaves fell from the trees,
                                            the stars fell from the sky
Like snowflakes, slowly and vast:

79

As I walked through the lightfall, my footprints like small, even
    voids
Behind me,
                the color of starflakes settling on everything,
Light up to my ankles, then up to my knees,
I moved effortlessly through the splendor drifting around me
Until I became a dot,
                then grained out into light,
The voids of my footprints still sunk, hard-edged and firm, where
    I'd passed.

In my last dream, just before sunrise,
I showed slides, two slides at a time,
                of the Resurrection, one
A painting, the other a photograph.
Much later, I showed the Five Sorrows of the Virgin,
One at a time,
        three prayers of intercession and the Assumption of St. John . . .

The subject matter is not the persona, it's the person:
"If you licked my heart, you'd die,
                poisoned by gall and anxiousness."

Today, in mid-November's ocher afternoon light,
All's otherworldly,
                my neighbor rolling his garbage carts to the curb,
My son repacking the tulip bulbs in their black beds:
What stays important is what we don't know and what we are not,
For nothing and nothing make nothing.
                                —20 November 1985

—All my life I've stood in desire:

                            look upon me and leave me alone,
Clear my windows and doors of flies
And let them be, taking no heed of them: I abide
In darkness,

          it is so small and indivisible,
A full food, and more precious than time:

Better to choose for your love what you can't think,

                                 better
To love what may be gotten and held,
And step above what can be cast out and covered up:
The shorter the word, the more it serves the work of the spirit:
Tread it down fast,

            have it all whole, not broken and not undone.
                           —28 November 1985

—Last day of November, rain
Stringy and almost solid,

                 incessantly gathering darkness around it
At one in the afternoon across

                 the Long Island of the Holston:
Up-island, steam from the coal gasification plant
Of Tennessee Eastman Corporation melds
With the cloud cover and rain cover

                 halfway up Bays Mountain—
Sycamore trees, with their mace-like and tiny pendants
And chimes, bow out toward the south sluice of the South Fork
Where I stand, a twentieth century man on ground
Holy for over ten thousand years:

Across the river, the burial sites
                         have been bulldozed and slash-stacked
Next to Smith Equipment Company;
Behind me, the chain-linked and barbed-wire fence
Cuts under the power pylon
                         from one side of the island to the other,
Enclosing the soccer fields;
Rain is continuous as I turn
From the gray, cataracted eye
                         of a television set
Caught in a junk-jam of timber and plastic against the bank,
And walk back to the footbridge
I'd crossed the river on an hour and a half before:
Next to it, off to the left,
A rectangular block of marble, backed by slab-stone,
Had been inscribed:
                         Long Island of the Holston
Sacred Cherokee Ground Relinquished by Treaty
Jan. 7, 1806.
                    3.61 Acres Returned
To the Eastern Band of Cherokee Indians by
The City of Kingsport on July 16, 1976:
Wolf Clan, Blue Clan, Deer Clan, Paint Clan, Wild Potato Clan,
Long Hair Clan, Bird Clan:

Steam stacks, sycamores, brush harbor,
                         rain like the river falling . . .
                         —5 December 1985

—Late afternoon, blue of the sky blue
As a dove's neck, dove
Color of winter branches among winter branches,

82

Guttural whistle and up,

    December violets crooked at my feet,
Cloud-wedge starting to slide like a detached retina
Slanting across the blue

    inaction the dove disappears in.

Mean constellations quip and annoy

     next night against the same sky
As I seek out, unsuccessfully,
In Luke's spyglass Halley's comet and its train of ice:
An ordered and measured affection is virtuous
In its clean cause

    however it comes close in this life.
Nothing else moves toward us out of the stars,

     nothing else shines.
      —12 *December 1985*

—*I am poured out like water.*
Who wouldn't ask for that *lightning strike,*

     the dog's breath on your knee
Seductive and unrehearsed,
The heart resoftened and made apt for illumination,
The body then taken up and its ghostly eyes dried?
Who wouldn't ask for that light,

    that liquefaction and entry?

The pentimento ridge line and bulk
Of the Blue Ridge emerge

    behind the vanished over-paint
Of the fall leaves across the street,
Cross-hatched and hard-edged, deep blue on blue.
What is a life of contemplation worth in this world?

83

How far can you go if you concentrate,
                        how far down?

The afternoon shuts its doors.
The heart tightens its valves,
                        the dragon maple sunk in its bones,
The grass asleep in its wheel.
The year squeezes to this point, the cold
Hung like a lantern against the dark
                        burn of a syllable.
I roll it around on my tongue, I warm its edges . . .
                                    —25 December 1985

84

Light Journal

To speak the prime word and vanish
                              into the aneurysm
Unhealed and holding the walls open,
Trip and thump of light
                              up from the fingernails and through
The slack locks and stripped vessels
At last to the inarticulation of desire . . .

———————

What did I think I meant then, Greece, 1959:
                              Beauty is in the looking for it,
The light here filtered through silk,
The water moving like breathing,
Moving in turn to the tide's turn,
                              black thread through the water weave.

Whatever it was, I still mean it.

———————

Everyone stands by himself
                              on the heart of the earth,
Pierced through by a ray of sunlight:
And suddenly it's evening.

———————

It's odd what persists
                              slip-grained in the memory,
Candescent and held fast,
Odd how for twenty-six years the someone I was once has stayed
Stopped in the columns of light
Through S. Zeno's doors,
                              trying to take the next step and break clear

A Journal of One Significant Landscape

April again. Aries comes forth

and we are released

Into the bitter veins and vast line
Under the elm and apple wood.

The last of the daffodils

Sulphurs the half-jade grass

against the arbor vitae.

Better the bodying forth,

better the coming back.

I listen to what the quince hums,
Its music filling my ear

with its flushed certitude.

Wild onion narrows the latitudes.

I pale and I acquiesce.

Gravity empties me

Stem by stem through its deep regalia,
Resplendent and faintly anodyne,
The green of my unbecoming

urging me earthward.

I long to escape through the white light in the rose root,
At ease in its clean, clear joy:
Unlike the spring flowers, I don't unfold, one petal

after another, in solitude—

Happiness happens, like sainthood, in spite of ourselves.

The day dies like a small child,
                              blushed and without complaint,
Its bedcovers sliding quietly to the floor.
How still the world's room holds,
                              everything straining its breath
In exhilaration and sadness.

Halfway through May and I am absolved,
A litter of leaves like half notes
                              held tight in the singing trees.
Against the board fence, the candle tips of the white pines
Gutter and burn, gutter and burn
                              on the blue apse of the sky.

How do we get said what must be said,
Seep of the honeysuckle like bad water, yellow
And slick, through the privet hedge,
                              tiger iris opening like an eye
Watching us steadily now, aware that what we see

In its disappearance and inexactitude
Is not what we think we see.
                         How does one say these things?
The sheathed beaks of the waxed magnolia
Utter their couched syllables,

Shhh of noon wind mouthing the last word.
Deep in the crevices and silk ravines of the snow rose,

Under the purple beards at the lily's throat,

                          silence stocks its cocoon:
Inside, in its radiance,

             the right answer waits to be born.

––––––––

Truthful words are not beautiful,

                  beautiful words not truthful,
Lao-tzu says. He has a point
Nor are good words persuasive:
The way of heaven can do no real harm,

               and it doesn't contend.

––––––––

Beginning of June, clouds like medieval banderoles
Out of the sky's mouth

             back toward the east,
Explaining the painting as Cimabue once did
In Pisa, in tempera,

           angels sending the message out

In those days. Not now, down here
Where the peaches swell like thumbs, and the little apples and
    pears
Buzz like unbroken codes on the sun's wire,

                  their secret shoptalk
The outtakes we would be privy to,

But never are, no matter how hard we look at them or listen.
Still, it's here in its gilt script,

             or there, speaking in tongues.
One of the nondescript brown-headed black birds that yawp

And scramble in and out of the trees
                            latches me with his lean eye

And tells me I'm wasting my time,
                            something I'm getting used to
In my one life with its one regret
I keep on trundling here
                    in order to alter it.
You're wasting your time, he tells me again, And I am.

───────────

It is not possible to read the then in the now.
It is not possible to see the blood in the needle's eye,
Sky like a sheet of carbon paper
                            repeating our poor ills
On the other side.
                    We must be good to each other.

───────────

Like a developing photograph,
                            the dawn hillsides appear
Black-and-white then green then rack-over into color
Down-country along the line,
House and barn as the night blanks
                            away into morning's fixer . . .

Like dreams awaiting their dreamers, cloud-figures step forth
Then disappear in the sky, ridge lines are cut,
                            grass moans
Under the sun's touch and drag:
With a sigh the day explains itself, and reliefs into place . . .

Like light bulbs, the pears turn on,
                              birds plink, the cow skull spins and stares
In heaven's eye, sunshine
Cheesecloths the ground beside the peach trees.
The dragon maple shivers its dry sides . . .

I put down these memorandums of my affections,
As John Clare said,
                         memory through a secondary
Being the soul of time
                         and life the principal but its shadow,
July in its second skin glistering through the trees . . .

                    _____

For the Heavenly Father desires that we should see,
Ruysbroeck has told us,
                         and that is why
He's ever saying to our innermost spirit one deep
Unfathomable word,
                         and nothing else . . .

                    _____

Thus stone upon stone,
And circle on circle I raised eternally:
So step after step
I drew back in sure ascension to Paradise,

Someone once wrote about Brunelleschi—
                              Giovanbattista Strozzi,
Vasari says—when he died

Vaulting the double dome of S. Maria del Fiore
In Florence,
            which everyone said was impossible.

Paolo Uccello, on the other hand, once drew
The four elements as animals·
                        a mole for earth,
A fish for water, a salamander for fire, and for air
A chameleon which lives on air
                        and thus will assume whatever color.

In his last days, secluded inside his house, he stayed up
All night in his study, his wife said,
                        intent on perspective.
O what a lovely thing perspective is, he'd call out.

August thrusts down its flushed face,
                        disvectored at the horizon.

                    ———————

How is the vanishing point
                when you look at it hard?
How does it lie in the diamond zones?
What are the colors of disappearance,
                        pink and gray,
Diamond and pink and gray?
                How are they hard to look at?

                    ———————

September's the month that moves us
                out of our instinct:

As the master said:

                   for knowledge, add something everyday,
To be wise, subtract . . .
This is the season of subtraction,

When what goes away is what stays,

                             pooled in its own grace,
When loss isn't loss, and fall
Hangs on the cusp of its one responsibility,
Tiny erasures,
              palimpsest over the pear trees.

Somewhere inside the landscape
Something reverses.
                 Leaf lines recoil, the moon switches
Her tides, dry banks begin to appear
In the long conduits
                 under the skin and in the heart.

I listen to dark October just over the hill,
I listen to what the weeds exhale,
                     and the pines echo,
Elect in their rectitude:
The idea of emptiness is everything to them.
                         I smooth myself, I abide.

Chinese Journal

In 1935, the year I was born,
                              Giorgio Morandi
Penciled these bottles in by leaving them out, letting
The presence of what surrounds them increase. The presence
Of what is missing,
                    keeping its distance and measure.

———————

The purple-and-white spike plants
                                  stand upright and spine-laced,
As though poised to fight by keeping still.
Inside their bristly circle,
The dwarf boxwood
                  flashes its tiny shields at the sun.

———————

Under the skylight, the Pothos plant
Dangles its fourteen arms
                          into the absence of its desire.
Like a medusa in the two-ply, celadon air,
Its longing is what it grows on,
                                 heart-leaves in the nothingness.

———————

To shine but not to dazzle.
Falling leaves, falling water,
                              everything comes to rest.

What can anyone know of the sure machine that makes all things
    work?
To find one word and use it correctly,
                    providing it is the right word,
Is more than enough:
An inch of music is an inch and a half of dust.

Night Journal II

The breath of What's-Out-There sags
Like bad weather below the branches,

                                     topsoiled, Venetian,
Trailing its phonemes along the ground.
                                       It says what it has to say

Carefully, without sound, word
After word imploding into articulation
And wherewithal for the unbecome.
                                    I catch its drift.

And if I could answer back,
If once I had a cloudier tongue,
                               what would I say?
I'd say what it says: nothing, with all its verities
Gone to the ground and hiding:
                               I'd say what it says now,
Dangling its language like laundry between the dark limbs,
Just hushed in its cleanliness.

The absolute night backs off.
                              Hard breezes freeze in my eyelids.
The moon, stamped horn of fool's gold,
Answers for me in the arteries of the oak trees.
I long for clear water, the silence
Of risk and deep splendor,
                              the quietness inside the solitude.
I want its drop on my lip, its cold undertaking.

Notes

Night Journal

Teaching a Stone to Talk, Annie Dillard (Harper & Row, 1982).

A Journal of the Year of the Ox

Catullus Tibullus and Pervigilium Veneris (Harvard University Press MCMLXXVI); *The Penguin Book of Italian Verse* (Penguin Books, 1960); *Historical Sketches of the Holston Valleys* by Thomas W. Preston (The Kingsport Press, 1926); "By the Banks of the Holston" by Jeff Daniel Marion, *The Iron Mountain Review*, Vol. 1, #2 (Winter 1984); *Il Palazzo di Schifanoia* by Ranieri Varese, Grafici Editoriale s.r.i. (Bologna, 1983); *The Cloud of Unknowing: An English Mystic of the 14th Century* (Burns Oates).

Light Journal

Salvatore Quasimodo, "Ed è súbito sera."

A Journal of One Significant Landscape

Lives of the Artists by Giorgio Vasari, translated by George Bull (Penguin Books, 1965).

Night Journal II

For Stanley Kunitz.